Christmas Carols
MUSIC
Activity Book

An Introduction to Music

Compiled and Edited by Sharon Stosur

ISBN 978-1-70510-294-7

HAL•LEONARD®

Visit Hal Leonard Online at
www.halleonard.com

Contact us:
Hal Leonard
7777 West Bluemound Road
Milwaukee, WI 53213
Email: info@halleonard.com

In Europe, contact:
Hal Leonard Europe Limited
42 Wigmore Street
Marylebone, London, W1U 2RN
Email: info@halleonardeurope.com

In Australia, contact:
Hal Leonard Australia Pty. Ltd.
4 Lentara Court
Cheltenham, Victoria, 3192 Australia
Email: info@halleonard.com.au

Hi! We're Cinnamon and Gumdrop, and this is the **Christmas Carols Music Activity Book**. If you're new to reading music and playing the piano, that's okay! We'll start at the beginning. Rudolph, Santa and Mrs. Claus, and all our friends at the North Pole will be here to help. We'll learn about music and play and sing some of your favorite Christmas carols. In addition to the carols there are plenty of games, puzzles, and other activities to enjoy. Let's get started!

Christmas Carols
MUSIC
Activity Book

❧ **An Introduction to Music** ❧

Contents

The Staff

When people sing or play music on an instrument, the sound they make can be written down with musical symbols called **notes**. Notes can be put together one by one to make a song.

To make it easier to see which notes are higher or lower than others, music notes are written on a set of five lines and four spaces called a **staff**. At the beginning of the staff is a **clef sign** to name the lines and spaces. The clef sign we use in this book is called **Treble Clef**.

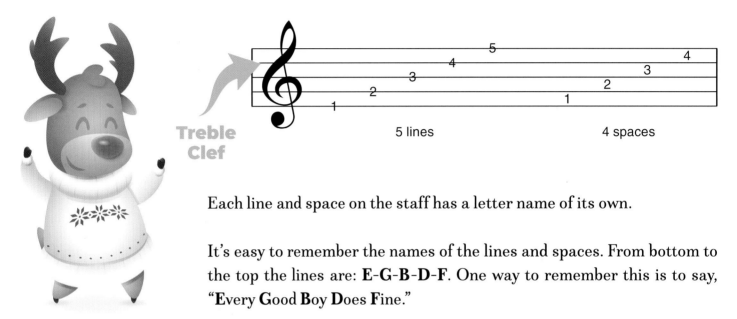

Treble Clef

5 lines   4 spaces

Each line and space on the staff has a letter name of its own.

It's easy to remember the names of the lines and spaces. From bottom to the top the lines are: **E-G-B-D-F**. One way to remember this is to say, "**E**very **G**ood **B**oy **D**oes **F**ine."

From bottom to top the spaces are: **F-A-C-E**. This is easy to remember because the names of the spaces spell "face."

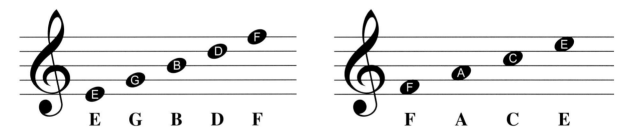

E   G   B   D   F   F   A   C   E

If a note is too high or too low to fit on the staff, extra lines can be added. These short lines are called **ledger lines**.

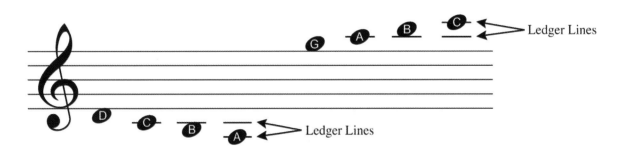

4

Notes on the Staff

Use notes on the staff to spell words. Place the notes on the correct line or space.
The first one is done for you.

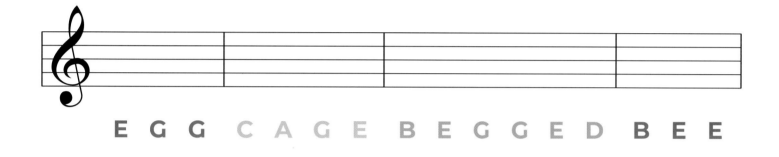

B E D   **C A G E D**   C A B   C A F E

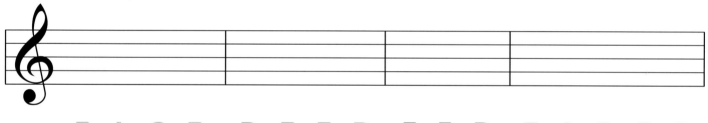

E G G   C A G E   B E G G E D   **B E E**

F A C E   D E E D   **F E D**   F A D E D

Answers on page 72

The Keyboard

It's easy to play notes on the piano keyboard. The keyboard is organized in groups of black keys and white keys. Take a look at the keyboard below to see the pattern of black key groups.

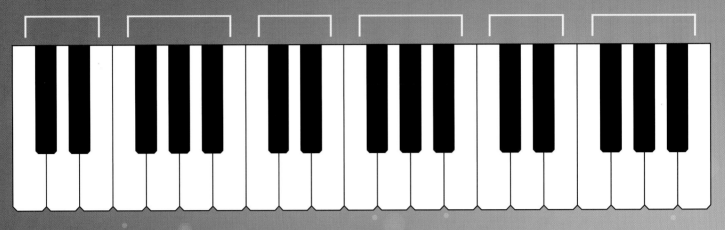

The white keys are named just like the notes on the staff, using the seven letters of the music alphabet.

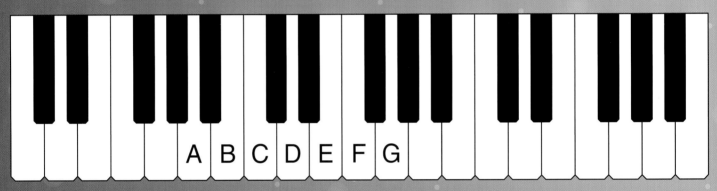

Name the Keys

Practice naming the white keys on the keyboards below.

Label all the Cs, Ds, and Es. These notes touch the groups of two black keys.

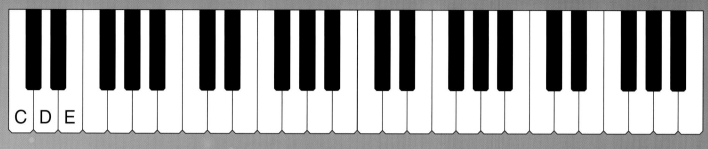

Label all the Fs, Gs, As, and Bs. These notes touch the groups of three black keys.

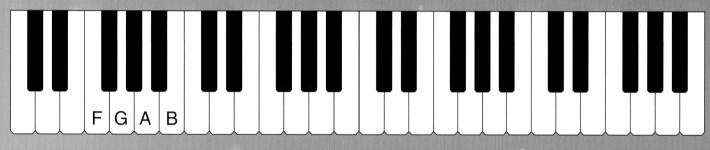

Fill in the names of the missing keys:

Finger Numbers

Finger numbers tell us which finger to use when we play notes on the keyboard. We number the fingers 1–5, and thumb is always number 1.

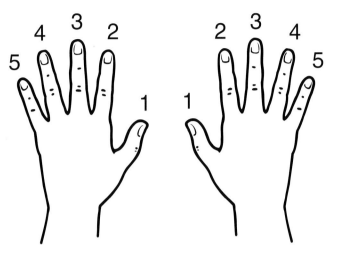

Left Hand (L.H.)   Right Hand (R.H.)

Play "Jingle Bells" using finger numbers. Place your right-hand thumb on G, as illustrated on this small keyboard. Remember, G is found near the group of three black keys. Begin playing B with finger 3.

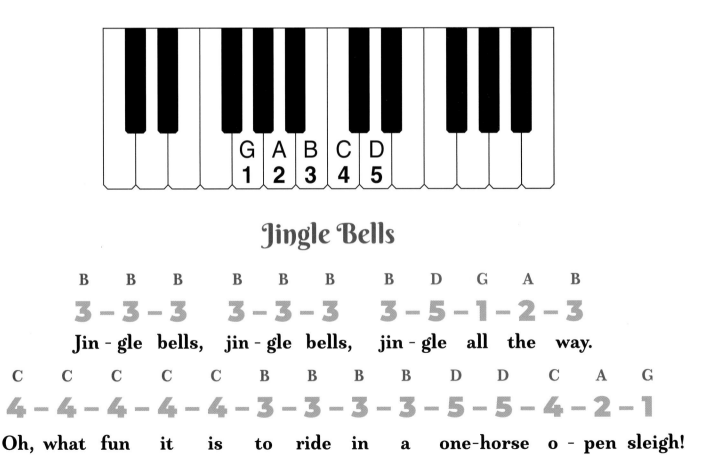

Jingle Bells

B	B	B		B	B	B		B	D	G	A	B
3	–	3	–	3	3	–	3	–	3	3	–	5	–	1	–	2	–	3

Jin - gle bells, jin - gle bells, jin - gle all the way.

C	C	C	C	C	B	B	B	B	D	D	C	A	G
4 – 4 – 4 – 4 – 4 – 3 – 3 – 3 – 3 – 5 – 5 – 4 – 2 – 1

Oh, what fun it is to ride in a one-horse o - pen sleigh!

Reading and Playing Music on the Staff

Here is the first line of "Good King Wenceslas." Remember the names of the lines and spaces or refer back to page 4 for a review. Be patient with yourself as you learn the names of the notes. And remember, the note names appear inside each note! There are small finger numbers above the notes. They tell you which fingers to use to play each note.

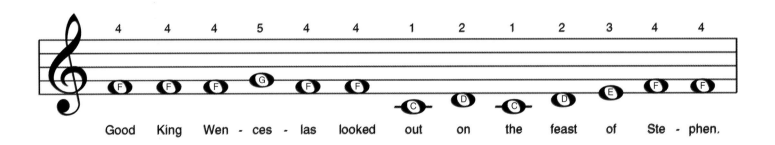

Note Values

A music note on a staff shows two things: how high or low a sound is, and how long the sound lasts.

Each type of note has a specific rhythmic value. Note values are measured in **beats**. When you tap your foot or clap your hands along with a song, you are tapping or clapping the beat.

When the quarter note gets one beat, all other rhythmic values are determined by the quarter note.

Quarter Note

A quarter note lasts for one beat.

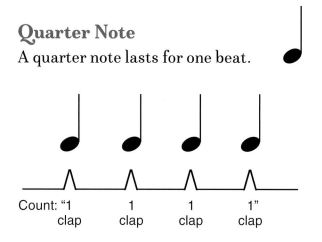

Count: "1   1   1   1"
       clap   clap   clap   clap

Half Note

A half note fills the time of two quarter notes.

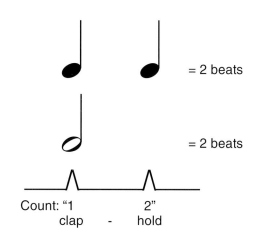

= 2 beats

= 2 beats

Count: "1   2"
       clap - hold

Dotted Half Note

A dotted half note fills the time of three quarter notes.

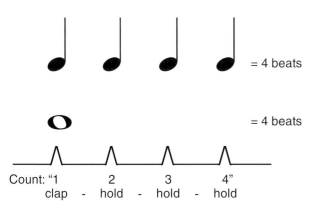

= 3 beats

= 3 beats

Count: "1   2   3"

clap - hold - hold

Whole Note

A whole note fills the time of four quarter notes.

= 4 beats

= 4 beats

Count: "1   2   3   4"

clap - hold - hold - hold

Here is the first line of "Good King Wenceslas" written in rhythm.

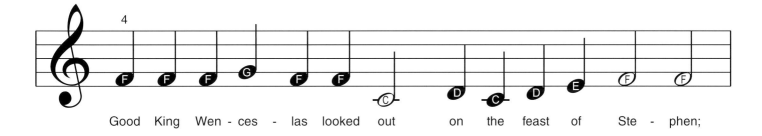

Coloring Fun

Use the note values to color Santa, Rudolph and Frosty.

If the note equals **4 beats**, color those areas **brown**.

If the note equals **3 beats**, color those areas **orange**.

If the note equals **2 beats**, color those areas **green**.

If the note equals **1 beat**, color those areas **red**.

How Music Is Organized

You already know about the staff, which shows you how high or low the notes are. Here's the staff with some added music symbols to help you read the notes. You'll always find a **clef** sign at the beginning of each line of music.

Bar lines divide the staff into **measures**, which contain groups of beats. Right next to the clef sign is a **time signature**. The top number tells you how many beats are in each measure. The number four on the bottom reminds you that a quarter note equals one beat. There is a **double bar line** at the end of the final measure. This sign tells you where the song ends.

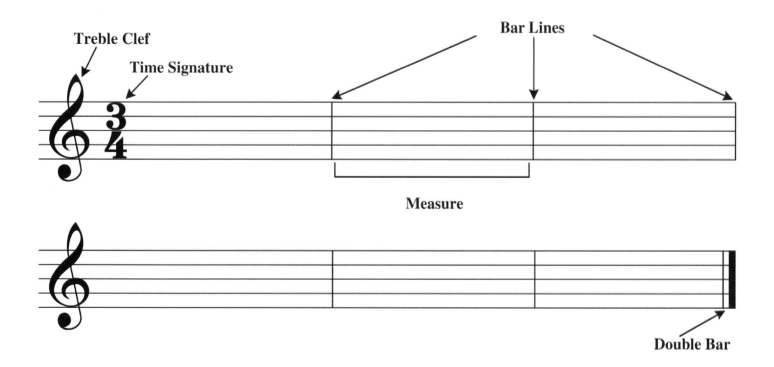

Counting Notes in 4/4 Time

"Jolly Old St. Nicholas" has a 4/4 **time signature**. The number 4 on top means there are four beats in each measure. Tap your foot or count along with the numbers "1-2-3-4" for each measure to make sure that you keep a steady beat.

Jolly Old St. Nicholas

Traditional 19th Century American Carol

4 beats per measure

Add the Missing Bar Lines

Bar lines divide music into **measures**. The **time signature** tells us how many beats are in each measure.

First, note the time signature in each example. How many beats should be in each measure? Divide each example into measures using bar lines.

Intervals

When notes on the staff move from a line to a space, or a space to a line, we describe that distance in intervals. An **interval** is the distance between two notes on the staff or keyboard.

On the keyboard, a **2nd** (sometimes called a **step**) is the distance from one key to the very next key. Steps can move up or down. On the staff, a 2nd is written from a line to the very next space, or from a space to the very next line, up or down.

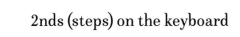

2nd
(step)

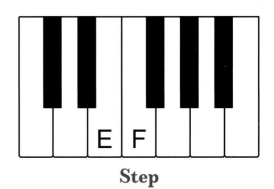

Step

A **3rd** (sometimes called a **skip**) on the staff moves from a line to a line, or a space to a space. On the keyboard, to play a 3rd, *skip* a key, moving up or down.

3rd
(skip)

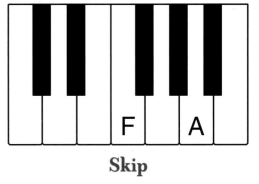

Skip

2nds (steps) on the keyboard

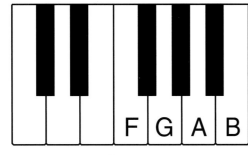

Steps

3rds (skips) on the keyboard

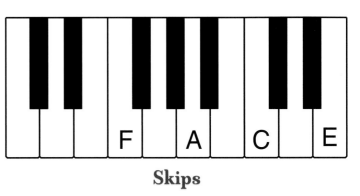

Skips

Larger intervals are notated in the same way. Use the keyboard diagram below to practice playing intervals on your keyboard.

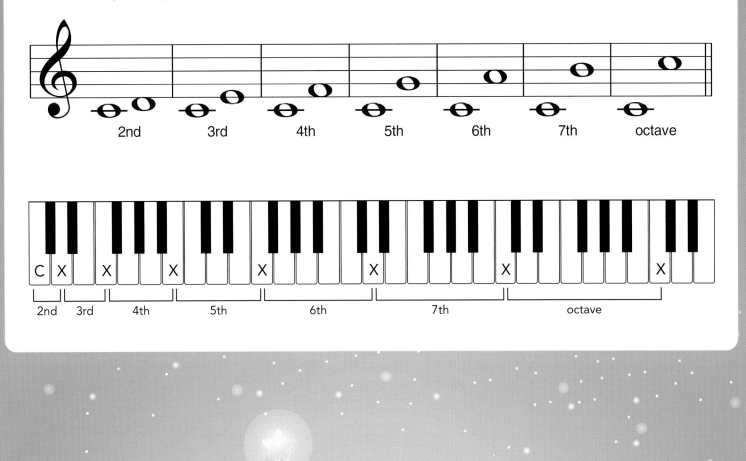

The Huron Carol

There are many 2nds (steps) in "The Huron Carol" and many other intervals too. The intervals are marked for you. Attention to intervals and noticing when the notes move up or down the staff will help you become skilled in reading music.

Traditional French-Canadian Text
Traditional Canadian-Indian Melody

Flats

As you know, there are both white and black keys on the piano keyboard. So far, we've been playing songs using only the white keys. Let's learn how to name the black keys and find them on the keyboard.

In the next song, "Good King Wenceslas," you'll see a note with a flat in front of it, like this:

A note with a flat in front of it is played a half step lower. A **half step** is a very small distance in music. On the keyboard, we describe it as one key to the very next key. Flat notes are usually between two musical letter names. For example, B-flat (B♭) is between A and B. This is easiest to see on the keyboard, where flat notes are usually black keys.

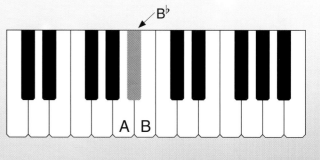

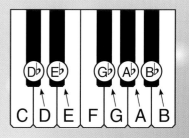

Remember, when you see a flat in front of a note, play or sing a half step lower. A note with a flat sounds a little lower than the same note without a flat.

Good King Wenceslas

Words by John M. Neale
Music from *Piae Cantiones*

More Music Signs and Symbols

RESTS

Rests are music symbols that stand for silence. A rest will indicate when *not* to play a note. Like notes, each rest is worth a certain number of beats, as shown below.

WHOLE REST	**HALF REST**	**QUARTER REST**
4 BEATS	2 BEATS	1 BEAT

Divide the rhythm below into measures. Count the value of the rests just like you would count notes.

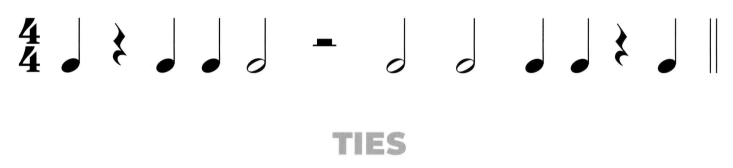

TIES

Earlier in the book you learned that a whole note is our longest note, and that it lasts four beats. Then how do composers write longer notes? One way is to use a **tie**. Ties are curved lines that connect two or more of the same note name to make longer notes over the bar line. The tied notes must be on the same line or in the same space. The first note is played or sung and held for the full value of all the tied notes. Play and count the example below.

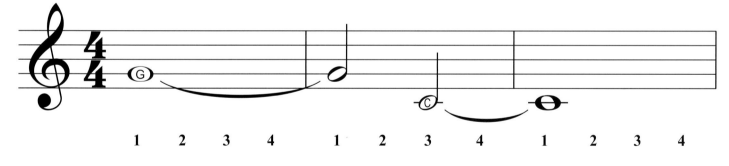

DYNAMICS

Dynamics are symbols for how softly or loudly music is played. Often the words are in Italian. Here are some common dynamics, and what they mean.

There are other symbols in music that help you play expressively. **Tempo markings** tell us about the speed and character of a song. These are found at the beginning of the song, right above the time signature.

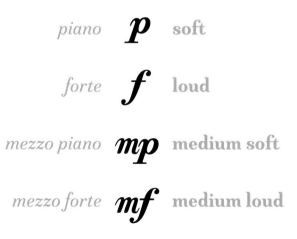

piano	*p*	soft
forte	*f*	loud
mezzo piano	*mp*	medium soft
mezzo forte	*mf*	medium loud

Bring a Torch, Jeannette, Isabella

Let's take a look at this playful French carol. The first two notes, C down to F is a 5th, followed by 2nds (steps).
In order to play the second measure easily, cross finger 2 **over** thumb and then back to F to continue playing up the keyboard.
This happens again in the next line. Read through the carol before you play, noticing the **quarter rests**. Remember,
a quarter rest has the same value as a quarter note. Because there is a **tie**, hold the last note six full beats.

Brightly

17th Century French Provençal Carol

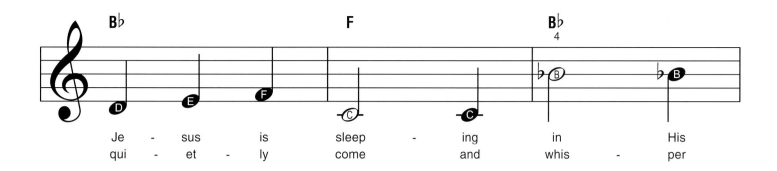

Je - sus is sleep - ing in His
qui - et - ly come and whis - per

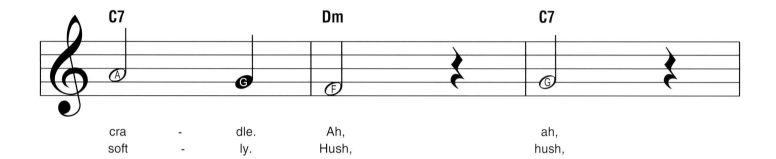

cra - dle. Ah, ah,
soft - ly. Hush, hush,

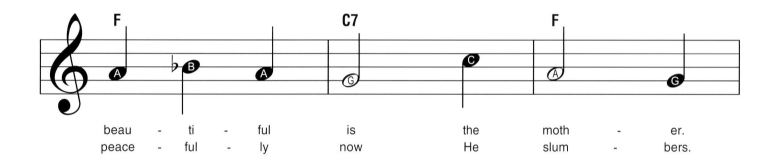

beau - ti - ful is the moth - er.
peace - ful - ly now He slum - bers.

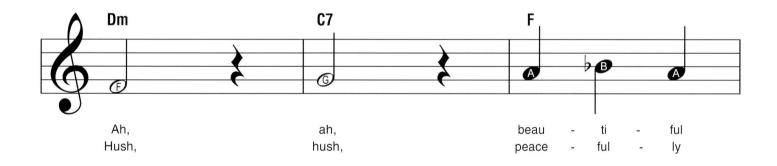

Ah, ah, beau - ti - ful
Hush, hush, peace - ful - ly

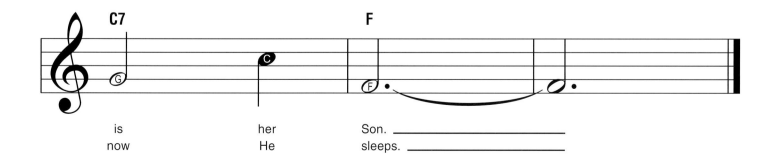

is her Son. _____
now He sleeps. _____

Sharps

G♯

Wait a minute! Can there be a sharp note and a flat note in the same song? Are you trying to get me mixed up?

Here's a new music symbol, the **sharp sign**: ♯ When placed in front of a note, it **raises** the note a half step.

Just like flats, sharp notes usually fall between two letter name notes. For example, G♯ is between G and A. On keyboard instruments, sharp notes are usually black keys.

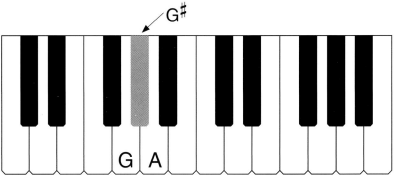

No, we're not trying to get Gumdrop mixed up. Black keys can be named either sharp or flat. Check out the keyboard below. The black keys get their name from the white keys.

Just remember: When you see a sharp in front of a note, play the very next note higher on the keyboard. when you see a flat in front of a note, play the very next note lower on the keyboard.

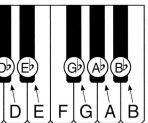

Coventry Carol

Look for two sharps in this carol, G♯ (between G and A)
and C♯ (between C and D).

Words by Robert Croo
Traditional English Melody

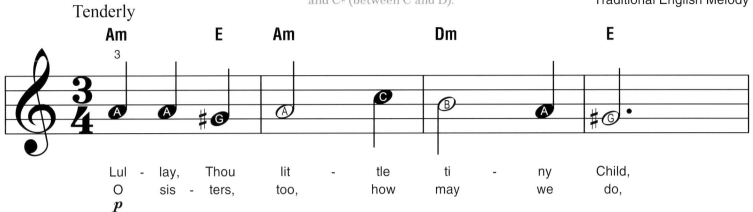

Tenderly

Lul - lay, Thou lit - tle ti - ny Child,
O sis - ters, too, how may we do,

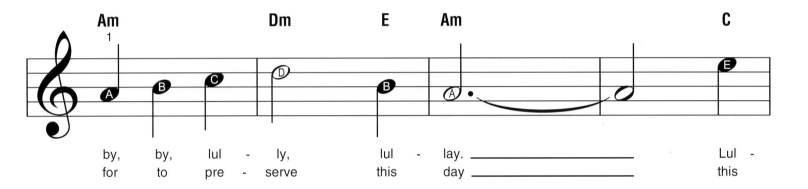

by, by, lul - ly, lul - lay. _____ Lul -
for to pre - serve this day _____ this

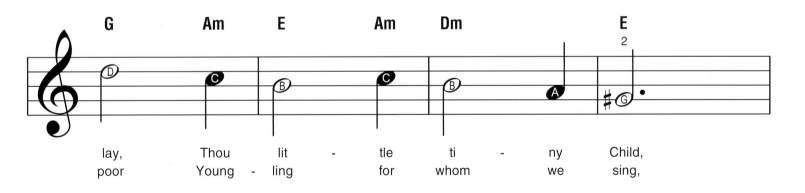

lay, Thou lit - tle ti - ny Child,
poor Young - ling for whom we sing,

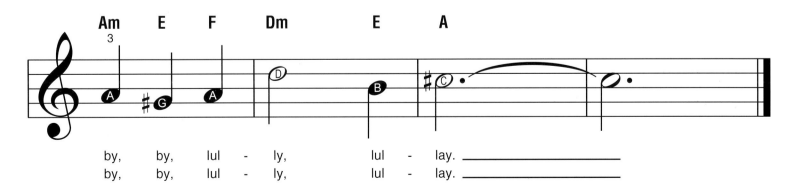

by, by, lul - ly, lul - lay. _____
by, by, lul - ly, lul - lay. _____

It Came Upon the Midnight Clear

This beautiful carol begins with a pick-up note. **Pick-up notes** are played before the first full measure of music. Notice the interval between G and E, gently stretching up to play the 6th, moving back to play B with finger 3. Notice the ties in lines 2, 4, 6, and 8, remembering to play the first note, and hold that note for the full value of both notes "tied" together. Check out the sharps in line 5, moving your fingers closer to the back of the keyboard to play F♯ and G♯.

Words by Edmund Hamilton Sears
Music by Richard Storrs Willis

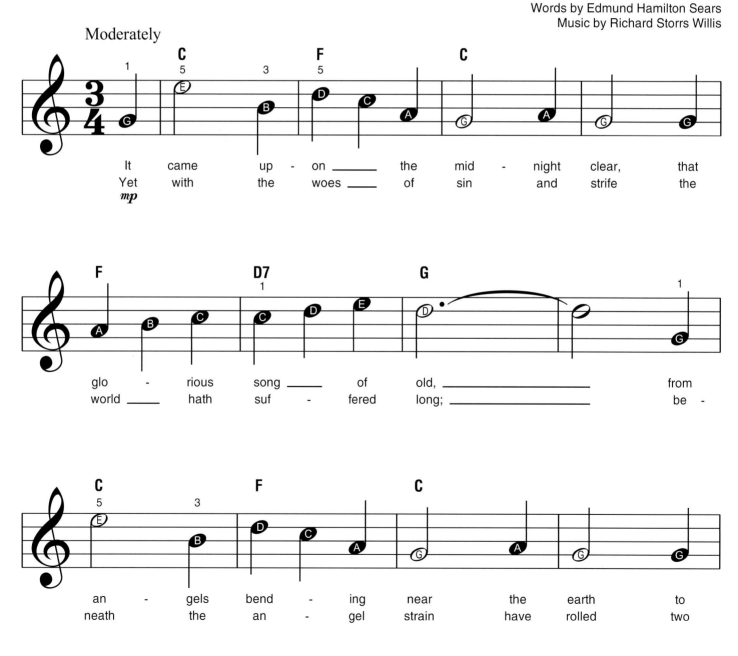

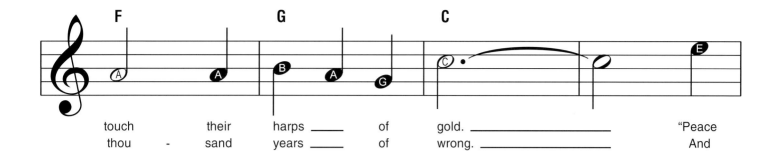

touch their harps ____ of gold. _____ "Peace
thou - sand years ____ of wrong. _____ And

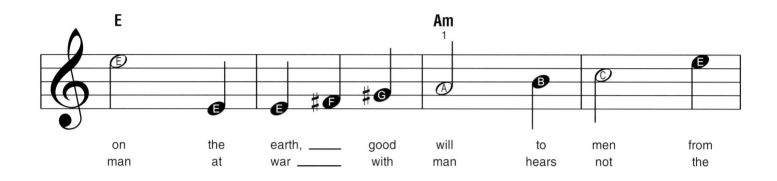

on the earth, ____ good will to men from
man at war ____ with man hears not the

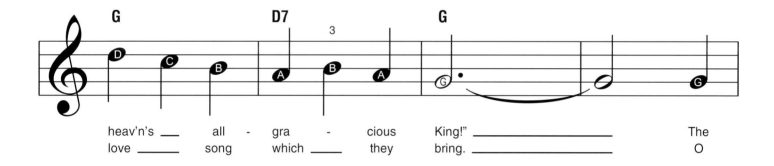

heav'n's ___ all - gra - cious King!" _____ The
love _____ song which ____ they bring. _____ O

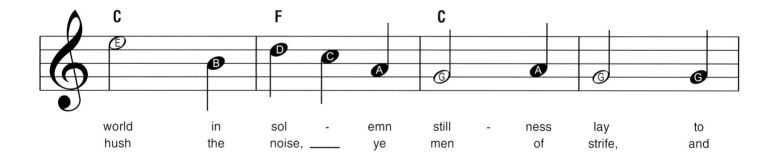

world in sol - emn still - ness lay to
hush the noise, ____ ye men of strife, and

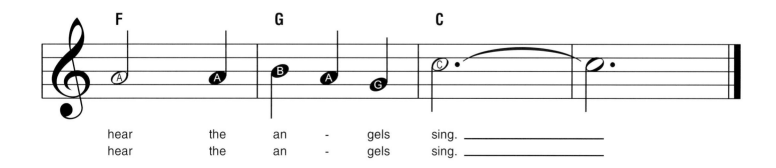

hear the an - gels sing. _____
hear the an - gels sing. _____

Sharp or Flat?

Placing a sharp in front of a note **raises** the pitch a half step. Add sharps to these notes. Be sure to place the sharp sign in front of the note. The "center square" of the sharp sign includes the line or space of the note.

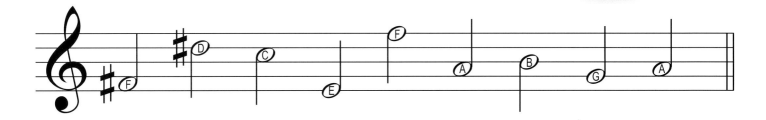

Placing a flat in front of a note **lowers** the pitch a half step. Add flat signs to these notes. Place the round part of the flat sign carefully to include the line or space of the note.

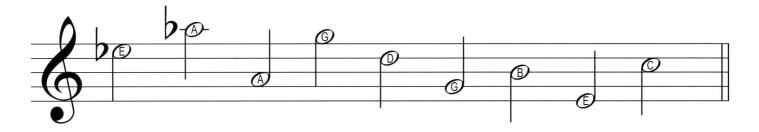

Name the following sharp and flat notes.

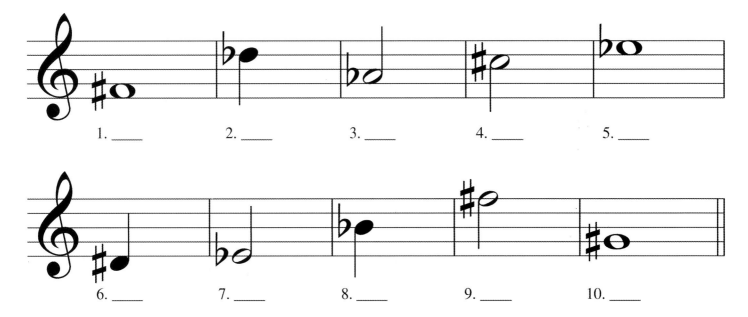

1. ____   2. ____   3. ____   4. ____   5. ____

6. ____   7. ____   8. ____   9. ____   10. ____

Answers on page 72

Note Reading Review

Name the notes and color Frosty the Snowman with crayons, pencils, or markers using the note and color key at the bottom of the page.

 orange   **black**   **brown**   **yellow**   **red**   **green**

What Child Is This?

This traditional English carol has a wide range. The melody spans from the D above middle C as high as high F, or the interval of a 10th. To play with a smooth and singing tone, pay careful attention to the fingering.

Words by William C. Dix
16th Century English Melody

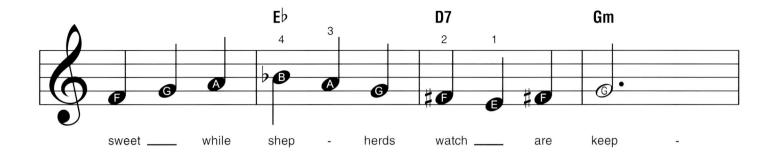

sweet ____ while shep - herds watch ____ are keep -

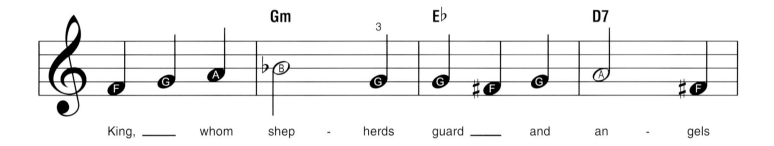

ing? This, this ____ is Christ the

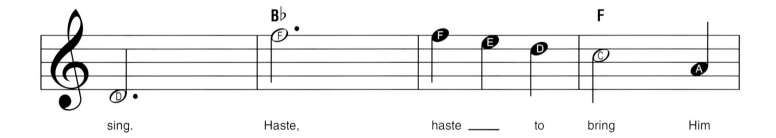

King, ____ whom shep - herds guard ____ and an - gels

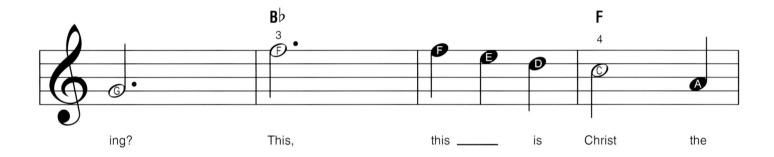

sing. Haste, haste ____ to bring Him

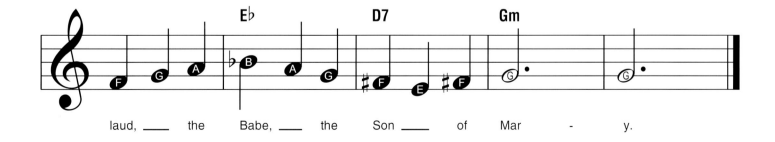

laud, ____ the Babe, ____ the Son ____ of Mar - y.

Eighth Notes

So far, you've learned about quarter notes, half notes, dotted half notes, and whole notes. Here's something new: eighth notes!

One eighth note looks like a quarter note with a flag. When two or more eighth notes appear together, the flags turn into beams. When the time signature is $\frac{4}{4}$, eighth notes are often connected in groups of two or four. The beams make reading the eighth notes easier.

Two eighth notes fill the time of one quarter note, or one beat.

32

When you count eighth notes and half beats, it's easier if you think about tapping your foot to the music. Look at Cinnamon's shoe, tapping along with the quarter notes. We count the quarter notes 1-2-3-4.

1   2   3   4

As Cinnamon taps, his foot moves up and down, tapping on the floor for each quarter note beat. To count eighth notes, he taps the same way but the notes sound twice as fast. Two eighth notes equal one quarter note.

Count: 1 & 2 & 3 & 4 &

The "ands" are when he raises his foot.

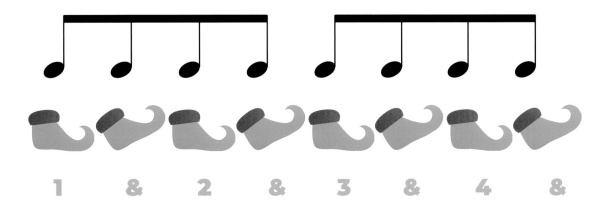

1   &   2   &   3   &   4   &

Try it yourself, tapping your foot and counting **1 & 2 & 3 & 4 &**

Clap and count the rhythm below from "Up on the Housetop."

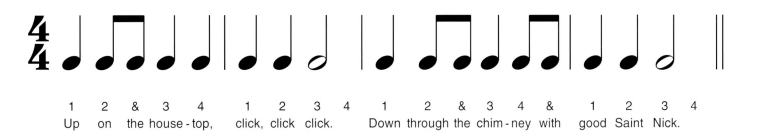

| 1 | 2 | & | 3 | 4 | 1 | 2 | 3 | 4 | 1 | 2 | & | 3 | 4 | & | 1 | 2 | 3 | 4 |
| Up | on | the | house- | top, | click, | click | click. | | Down | through | the | chim- | ney | with | good | Saint | Nick. | |

Hark! The Herald Angels Sing

Look ahead to the last two lines of this carol to find eighth notes.
Count, sing along, or tap your foot to help keep a steady beat.

Words by Charles Wesley
Music by Felix Mendelssohn-Bartholdy

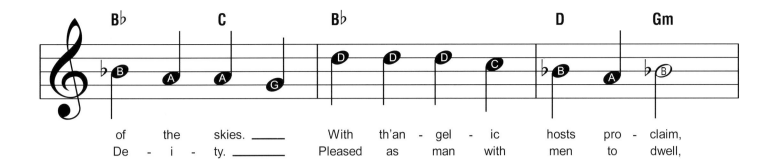
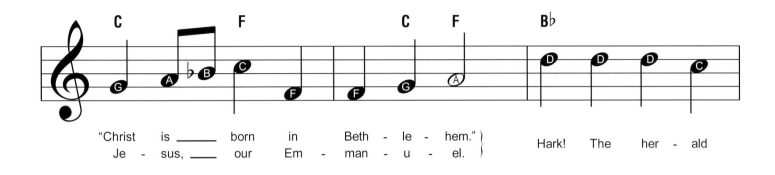

of the skies. _____ With th'an - gel - ic hosts pro - claim,
De - i - ty. _____ Pleased as man with men to dwell,

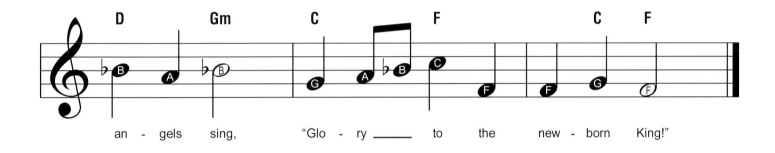

"Christ is _____ born in Beth - le - hem.")
Je - sus, ___ our Em - man - u - el.)

Hark! The her - ald

an - gels sing, "Glo - ry _____ to the new - born King!"

Interval Review

Circle the correct interval.

2nd or 3rd   3rd or 5th   6th or 7th   2nd or 4th   4th or 5th   5th or 6th

Draw intervals higher or lower, as indicated by the arrows.

↑ 3rd   ↓ 2nd   ↓ 3rd   ↑ 4th   ↑ 5th   ↓ 6th

Complete these measures from "The Huron Carol" by adding quarter notes as indicated.

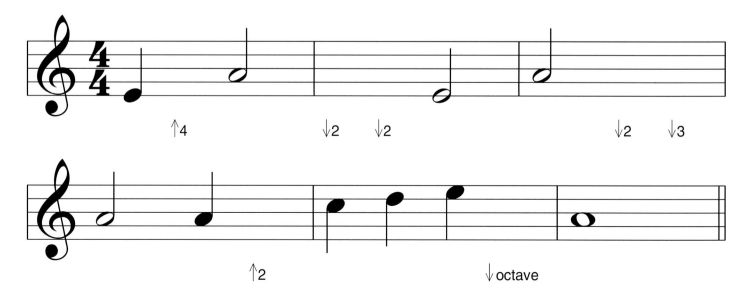

↑4   ↓2   ↓2   ↓2   ↓3

↑2   ↓octave

O Little Town of Bethlehem

Before you play this peaceful carol, look for the following intervals: 4th, 5th, 6th, and octave.

Words by Phillips Brooks
Music by Lewis H. Redner

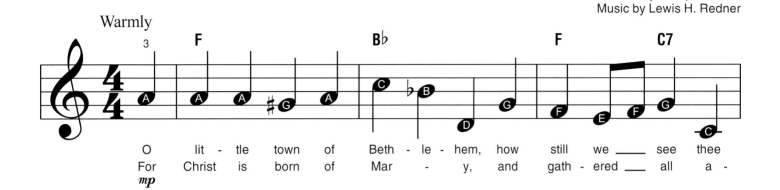

O lit - tle town of Beth - le - hem, how still we ____ see thee
For Christ is born of Mar - y, and gath - ered ____ all a -

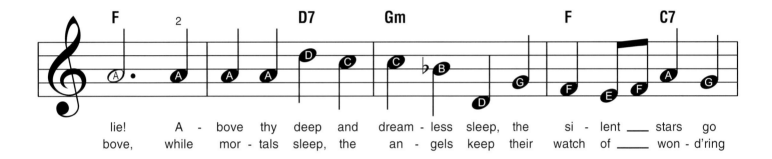

lie! A - bove thy deep and dream - less sleep, the si - lent ____ stars go
bove, while mor - tals sleep, the an - gels keep their watch of ____ won - d'ring

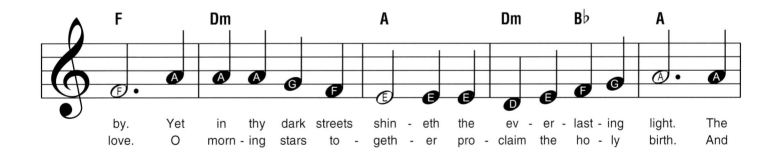

by. Yet in thy dark streets shin - eth the ev - er - last - ing light. The
love. O morn - ing stars to - geth - er pro - claim the ho - ly birth. And

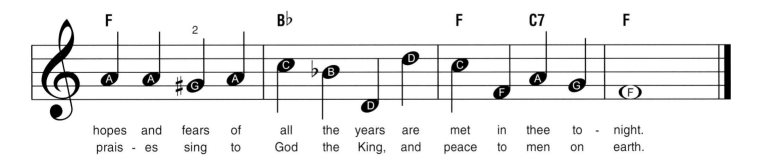

hopes and fears of all the years are met in thee to - night.
prais - es sing to God the King, and peace to men on earth.

Look ahead to the end of the song to see a new music symbol, the repeat sign. A **repeat sign** directs you to return to the beginning and play again. Notice the **1st and 2nd Ending brackets**. Play the music under the first bracket, repeat, and end by playing the music under the 2nd bracket.

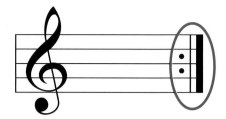

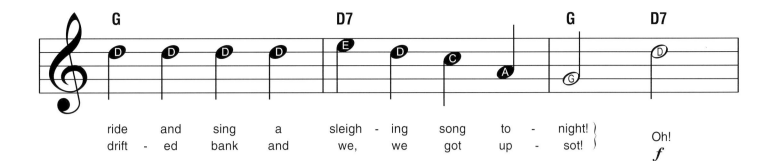

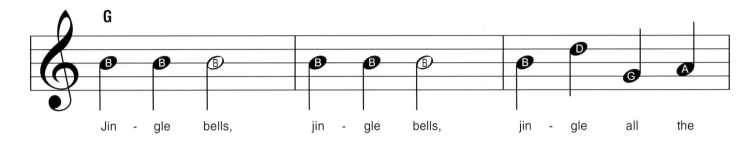

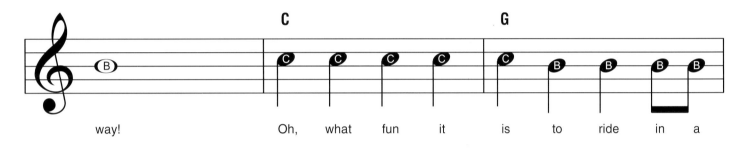

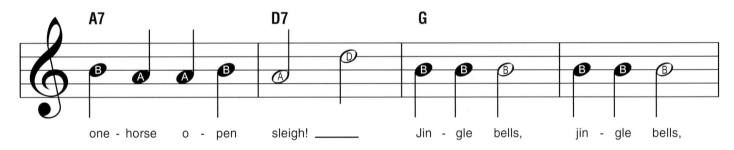

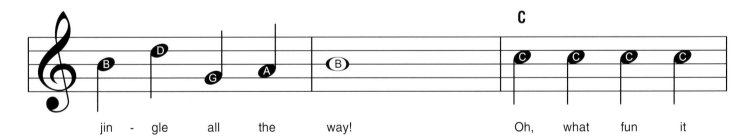

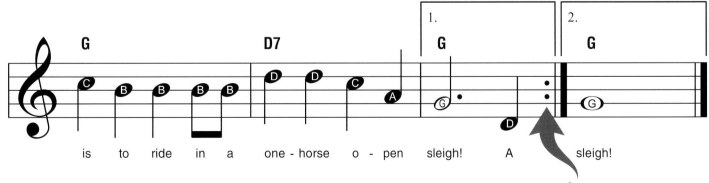

Repeat Sign (go back to the beginning and play again)

Crossword Fun

Across

1. The ____ half note lasts for three beats.

2. A whole note lasts ____ beats.

3. The ____ number of a time signature tells you how many beats are in a measure.

4. Adding a dot to a note ____ its value.

6. A ____ is a curved line that connects two notes with the same pitch.

7. A ____ is the space between two bar lines.

8. Two ____ notes take the time of one quarter note.

12. Notes that are too high or too low to fit on the staff are written using ____ lines.

14. The notes that fall in the four spaces of the treble clef spell ____.

15. Sharps ____ a note a half-step.

16. Notes are written on a ____ which has five lines.

Down

1. A _____ appears at the end of the final measure of a song. *(2 words)*

3. A ____clef appears at the beginning of a song.

4. The distance between two notes on the staff or keyboard is called an ____.

5. ____ are symbols that stand for silence.

9. Christmas songs or hymns are often called ____.

10. Flats ____ a note a half-step.

11. Eighth notes can be written with flags or ____.

13. A ____ note lasts two beats.

Answers on page 72

Up on the Housetop

Words and Music by
B.R. Hanby

Music Math

Let's do some music math! Add the values of the tied notes to find the answer to each of these musical equations. The first one is done for you. Check your answers on page 72.

1. ♩ + ♩ + ♩

   1 + 1 + 2 = 4

2. 𝅝 + 𝅝

   __ + __ = __

3. ♩ + ♩ + ♩

   __ + __ + __ = __

4. ♩ + ♩ + ♩

   __ + __ + __ = __

5. 𝅝 + ♩ + ♩

   __ + __ + __ = __

Circle **T** for True or **F** for False.

6. T F ♩ = ♫

7. T F ♪. + ♪ + ♪. + ♪ = ♩

8. T F 𝄽 + ♫ = ♩

9. T F 𝄽 + ♩ + ♩ = 𝅝

10. T F 𝄽 + 𝄽 + ♩ + 𝄽 = ♩.

42

The Holly and the Ivy

This beautiful English carol is easy to learn when you notice that the first eight measures are almost the same as the second eight measures. Can you find the differences? Study the intervals in the first two full measures. In measure 1, G up to E is a 6th, moving down a 2nd to D. How many times can you find this pattern?

Moderately slow

18th Century English Carol

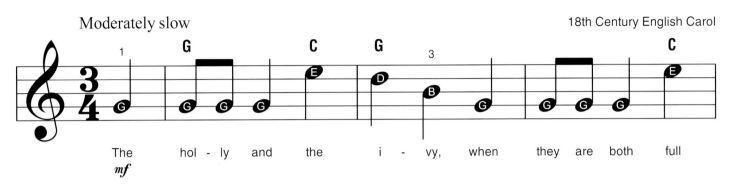

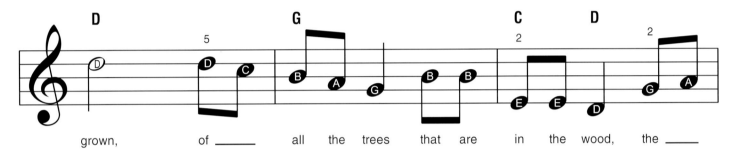

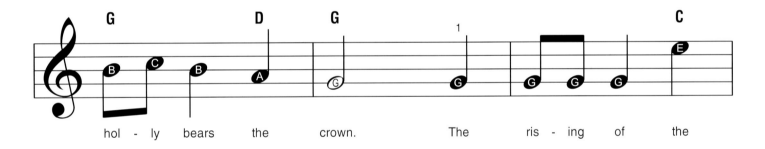

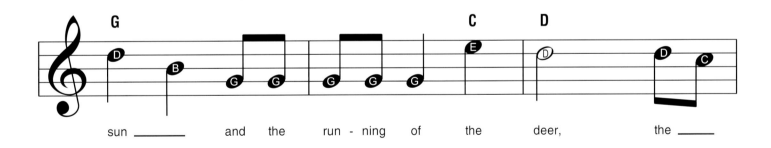

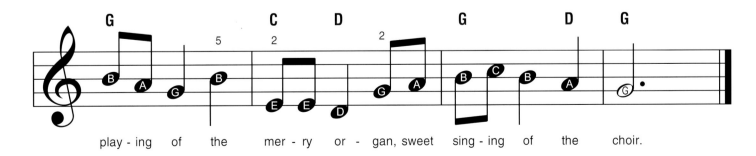

Dotted Notes

Another way to make a note last longer is to add a dot. Adding a dot to a note adds half the value of the note it follows. It's kind of like playing a tied note without the tie.

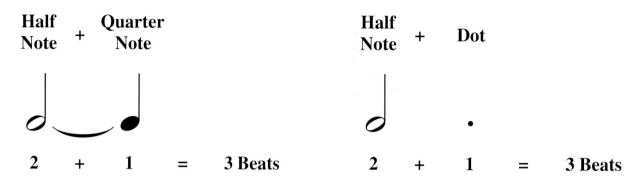

You can add a dot to any note to increase its value, if there are enough beats available in the measure. When you add a dot to a quarter note, you add half a beat.

A dotted quarter note is often followed by an eighth note.

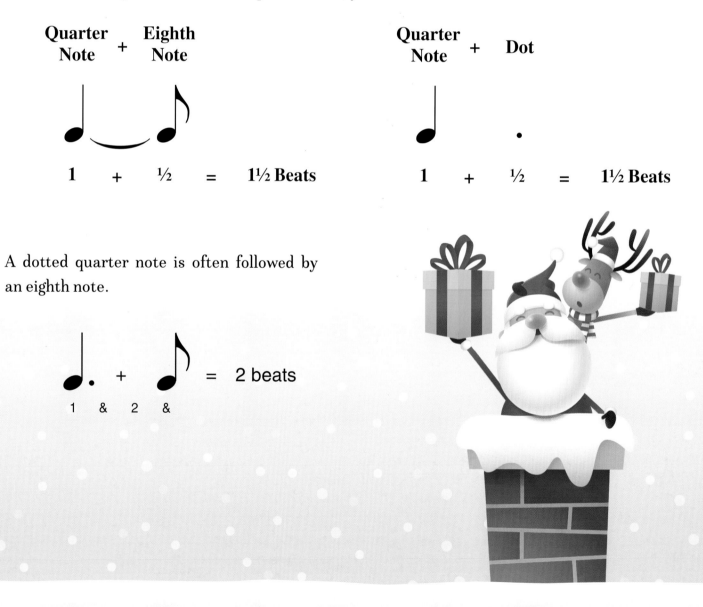

Here are some dotted quarter note rhythms. Clap and count each example. You may wish to tap your foot to keep the beat.

Silent Night

There are many dotted quarter note rhythms in "Silent Night." Count or sing as you play these rhythms the first few times. Be gentle with the eighth notes, keeping in character with this quiet carol.

Words by Joseph Mohr
Music by Franz X. Gruber

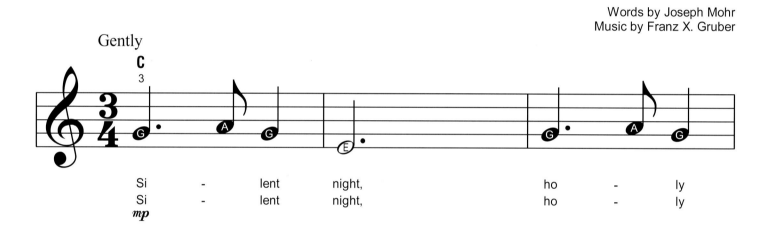

Si - lent night, ho - ly
Si - lent night, ho - ly

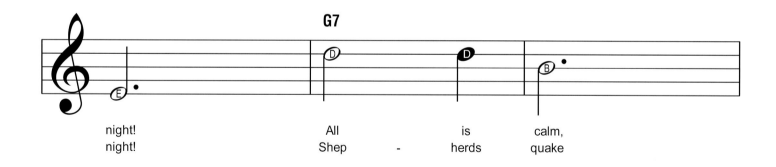

night! All is calm,
night! Shep - herds quake

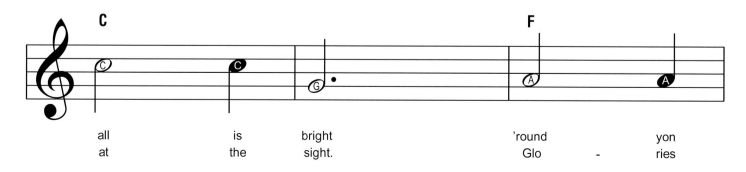

all is bright 'round yon
at the sight. Glo - ries

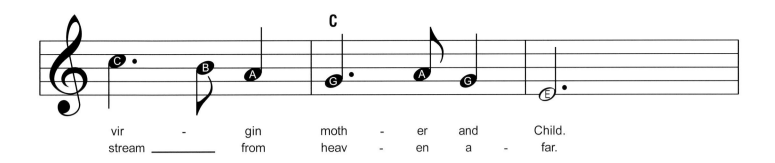

vir - gin moth - er and Child.
stream _____ from heav - en a - far.

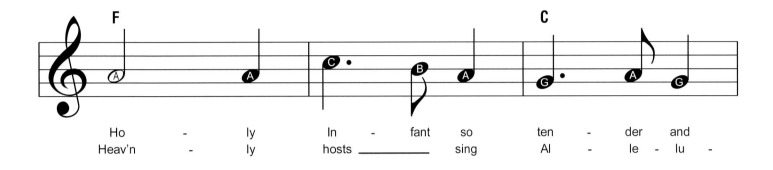

Ho - ly In - fant so ten - der and
Heav'n - ly hosts _____ sing Al - le - lu -

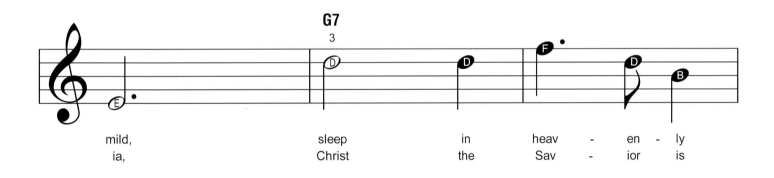

mild, sleep in heav - en - ly
ia, Christ the Sav - ior is

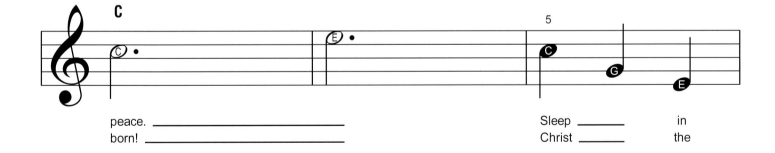

peace. _____ Sleep _____ in
born! _____ Christ _____ the

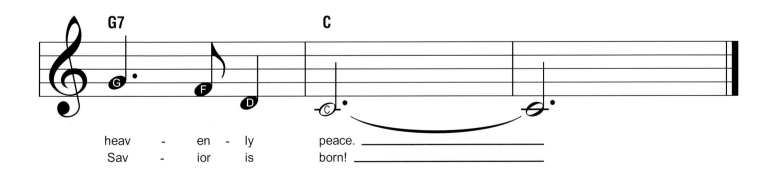

heav - en - ly peace. _____
Sav - ior is born! _____

Away in a Manger

Compare lines 1 and 3 in this famous carol, and you will see that they are the same, except for the pick-up note at the beginning.
This is helpful to know, as once you've learned the first line, you know half the song! Compare lines 2 and 4. Same or different?

Words by John T. McFarland (v.3)
Music by James R. Murray

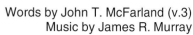

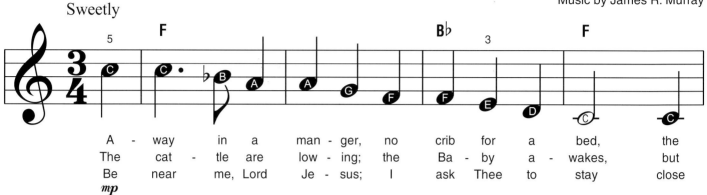

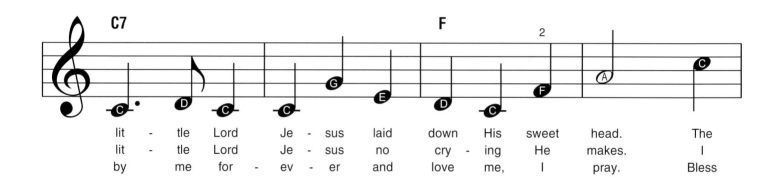

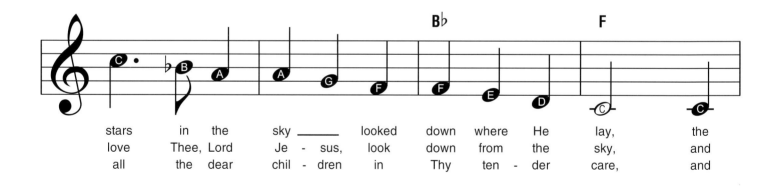

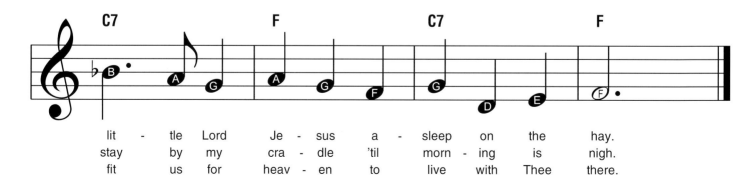

Rhythm Match

Match the song titles with the rhythm that fits. One is done as an example.

_1_ Jingle Bells

____ Up on the Housetop

____ What Child Is This?

____ O Come, All Ye Faithful

____ The Holly and the Ivy

____ Jolly Old St. Nicholas

____ Away in a Manger

____ Silent Night

Answers on page 72.

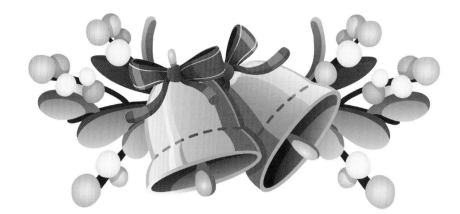

I Heard the Bells on Christmas Day

The thumb has an important role as you play this lovely carol with lyrics by the famous American poet Henry Wadsworth Longfellow. In the first full measure, substitute your thumb on B on beat 4, to move smoothly up the keyboard. From measure 3 to 4, cross thumb under C♯ as you continue to high G. Cross thumb under one last time in measure 7, to play B.

Words by Henry Wadsworth Longfellow
Music by John Baptiste Calkin

Joy to the World

Starting on the C above middle C, and moving down note by note to middle C (also known as a **scale** in music), the opening four measures make this famous carol easy to recognize. Use the fingering provided to play the scale patterns smoothly and skillfully.

Words by Isaac Watts
Music by George Frideric Handel

Joyfully

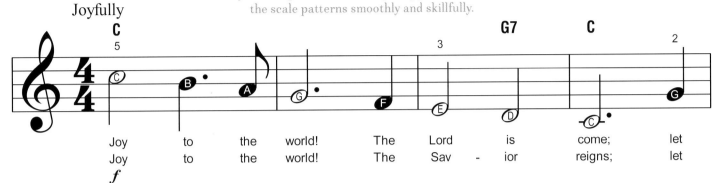

Joy to the world! The Lord is come; let
Joy to the world! The Sav - ior reigns; let

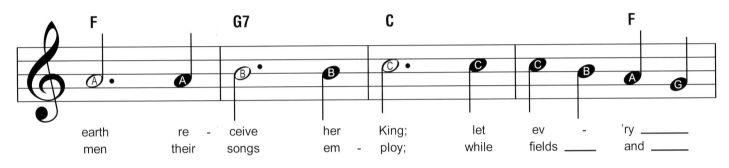

earth re - ceive her King; let ev - 'ry _____
men their songs em - ploy; while fields _____ and _____

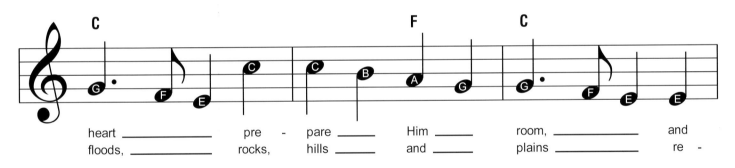

heart _____ pre - pare _____ Him _____ room, _____ and
floods, _____ rocks, hills _____ and _____ plains _____ re -

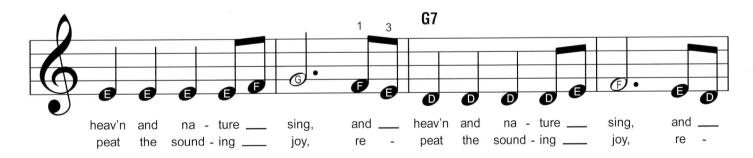

heav'n and na - ture _____ sing, and _____ heav'n and na - ture _____ sing, and _____
peat the sound - ing _____ joy, re - peat the sound - ing _____ joy, re -

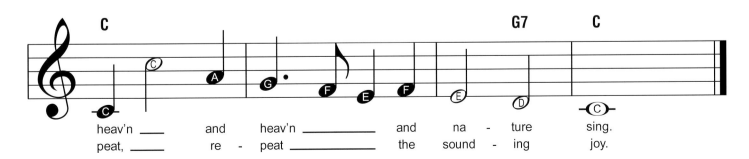

heav'n _____ and heav'n _____ and na - ture sing.
peat, _____ re - peat _____ the sound - ing joy.

Playing by Ear

Playing by ear is an important musical skill. Below, "O Come, All Ye Faithful" has several measures with missing quarter notes. Play the carol and add those missing notes, using your ear to tell you which notes to play. Later, fill in the notes on the staff. You can check your answers on page 72.

O Come, All Ye Faithful

Music by John Francis Wade
Latin Words translated by Frederick Oakeley

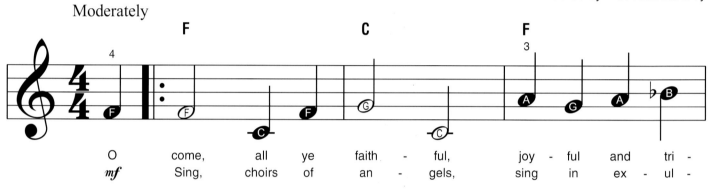

O come, all ye faith - ful, joy - ful and tri -
Sing, choirs of an - gels, sing in ex - ul -

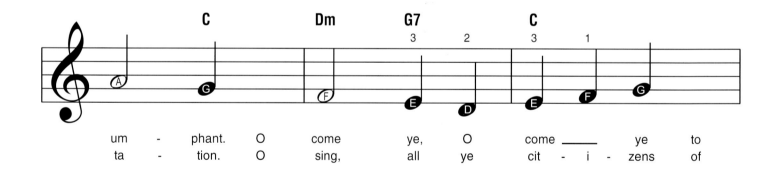

um - phant. O come ye, O come ____ ye to
ta - tion. O sing, all ye cit - i - zens of

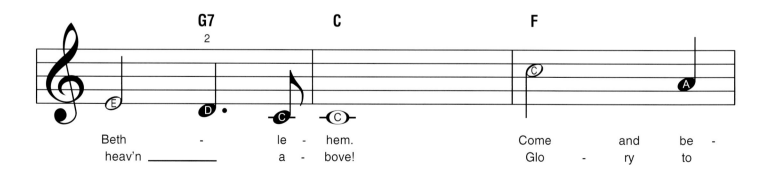

Beth - le - hem. Come and be -
heav'n ____ a - bove! Glo - ry to

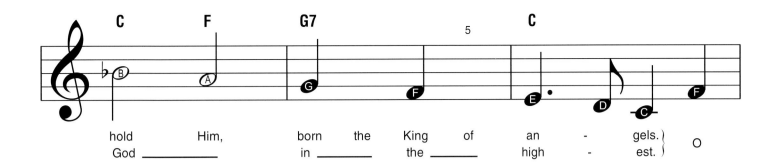

hold Him, born the King of an - gels. 〕 O
God _____ in _____ the _____ high - est. 〕

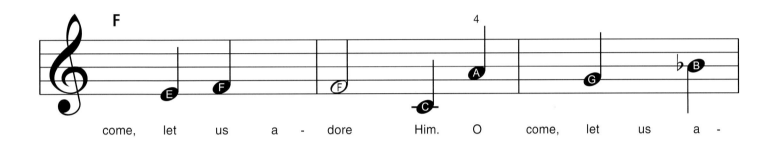

come, let us a - dore Him. O come, let us a -

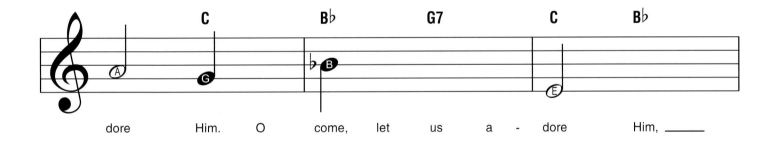

dore Him. O come, let us a - dore Him, _____

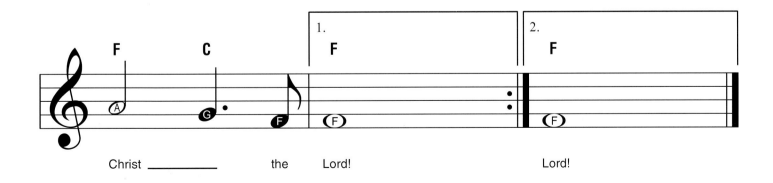

1.
Christ _____ the Lord!

2.
Lord!

Studying a piece of music before sight-reading it is a helpful way to learn a new song quickly. Before you play "The First Noël," let's take a close look at how it's constructed.

Most of the melody is step-wise, meaning the notes move in 2nds, one note to the next note, without skipping any keys. You'll find the first larger interval, a 4th (C down to G) in measure 7. That 4th appears three more times. Look for those places and circle the 4ths.

Compare the first eight measures with the second eight measures. Are they the same or different? Something interesting happens in the last eight measures. The melody begins as usual, then changes. Practice the measures that are new, and confidently play the whole piece from the beginning.

The First Noël

17th Century English Carol
Music from W. Sandys' *Christmas Carols*

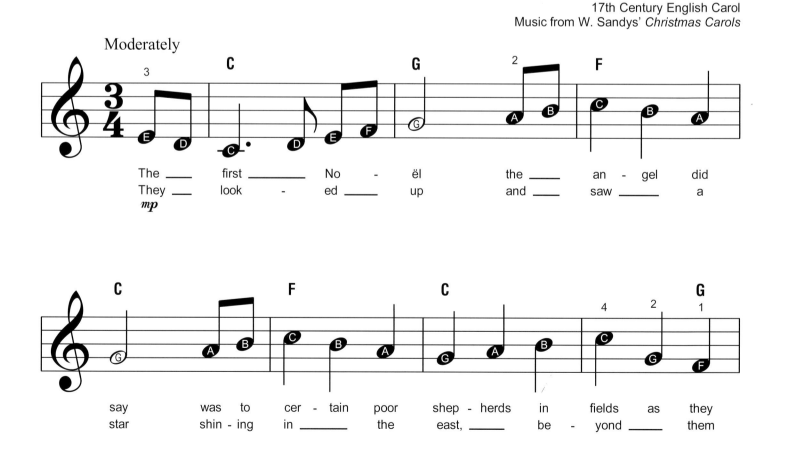

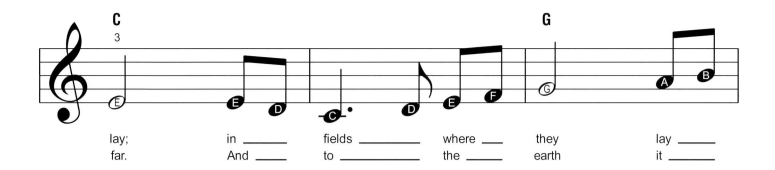

lay;   in _____ fields _____ where ___ they   lay _____
far.   And _____ to _____ the _____ earth   it _____

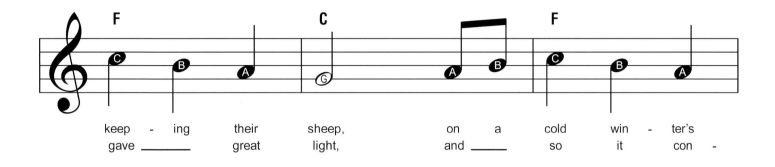

keep - ing their sheep,   on a cold win - ter's
gave _____ great light,   and _____ so it con -

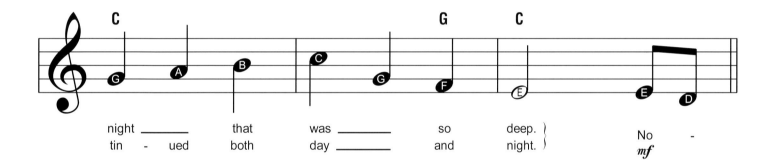

night _____ that was _____ so deep.   No -
tin - ued both day _____ and night.

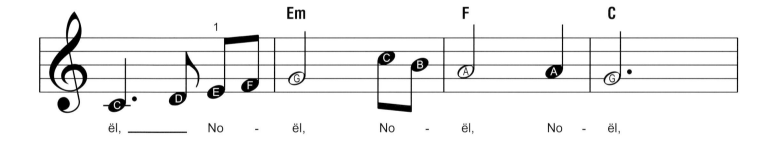

ël, _____ No - ël,   No - ël,   No - ël,

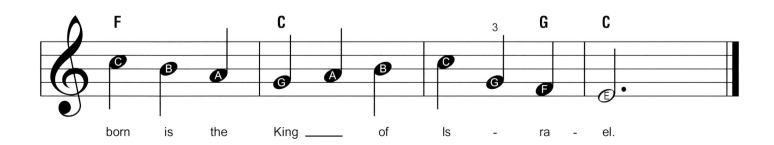

born is the King _____ of Is - ra - el.

Word Search

Can you find all the music words on the list? Circle the words you find and then cross them off the list as you work.

```
X U M E X D N O K E Y B O A R D X W K S T E P
Y B Z S P A C E C D O U B L E B A R H O R U O
I H A L F N O T E Q N M L E L Y R I Y U G F S
Q X Z I M C D J O L L Y I O K P E T T E E W I
W U B S U P I J N S G T B U W L A A N L S E O
D C A H S W Z J P W X M S E G X N I A E R X V
G R R R N Z W O R P Y Q V N I G L C T U P V F
N S L T T A M X T S Y A I N I R S O S B O W I
G J I I N E C G D W T J V S E L N A D T L J T
H B N V Q D R R U C Q C E G F O E B X G E J K
A O E D D D O N O I J M D Q E M T Y S H T W Q
S R S U X H J Q O Q I E D J X U R R A X G W L
H E O U C P O Z U T L U L O H A E S T A F F Q
A P I N T E R V A L E Q I E T B B Y L R R F E
R E F R W X X V J C P G T F M T L F J L W S I
P A D F H C A R O L G O Z U R Q E S T U B K C
D T V L O A M I N E N T N Y N X C D T S L I W
O S A A L C U F P H A R W Y Q I L G N Z C P Q
C I A T E E A R T E E L T G M A E U A O B N H
M G G P N I A H B G W S K A A G F A P M T A J
M N D I O Y G S N A E I N Z X A C M A Z C E O
M D L D T I L I N R C Y C N Q Z E W K O S J D
T V K S E R F Y A L D H Y U E T L B E A M X O
```

Arpeggio	**Dynamics**	**Jolly**	**Repeat sign**	**Step**
Bar lines	**Eighth note**	**Keyboard**	**Rest**	**Tempo**
Beam	**Finger numbers**	**Ledger line**	**Rit**	**Tie**
Beat	**Flag**	**Line**	**Scale**	**Time signature**
Carol	**Flat**	**Measure**	**Sharp**	**Treble clef**
Chord symbol	**Half note**	**Notes**	**Skip**	**Whole note**
Dotted note	**Interval**	**Octave**	**Space**	
Double bar	**Jingle**	**Quarter note**	**Staff**	

Answers on page 72.

O Come, Little Children

The lyrics for this German carol were inspired by the poem "The Children at the Manger" by Christoph von Schmid. Look through each line. How many 3rds did you notice? 3rds are easy to see as notes that move line to line, or space to space. Most of this carol stays in one place on the keyboard. The fingering in lines three and four will help you shift as needed in the last phrase.

Words by C. von Schmid
Music by J.P.A. Schulz

O Christmas Tree

This carol originally had little to do with Christmas. Instead of a decorated holiday tree, the lyrics spoke of the evergreen fir as a symbol of tradition and faithfulness. It became associated with Christmas as additional lyrics were added.

Traditional German Carol

Note Reading Challenge

The following measures below contain notes that spell a word.
Name the notes to discover the word.

__ __ R O L L __ L __ S __ __ S O N

J I N L __ L __ __ L L W __ N __ __ __ S L __ S

__ N __ __ L T R __ __ __

On the blank staff, create your own words.

1. _____ 2. _____ 3. _____ 4. _____ 5. _____

Answers on page 72.

Deck the Hall

Study the **form** (how the song is constructed) of this carol before you play.
Compare the first four measures with the next four measures. Are they the same or different?
Now compare these measures with the last four measures. Same or different? Different in what way?

Traditional Welsh Carol

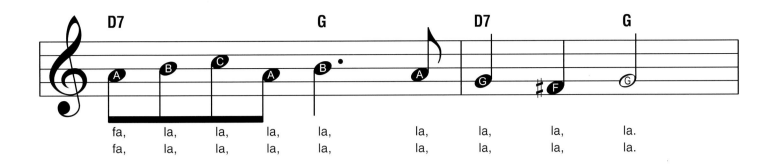

fa, la, la, la, la, la, la, la, la.
fa, la, la, la, la, la, la, la, la.

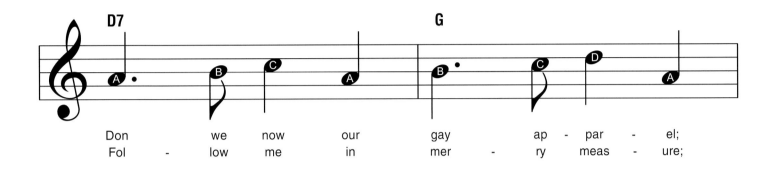

Don we now our gay ap - par - el;
Fol - low me in mer - ry meas - ure;

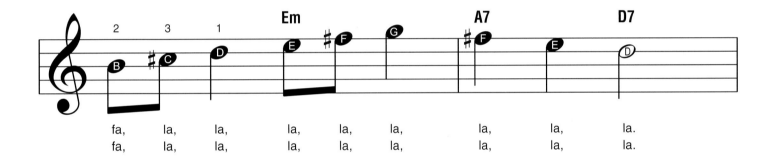

fa, la, la, la, la, la, la, la, la.
fa, la, la, la, la, la, la, la, la.

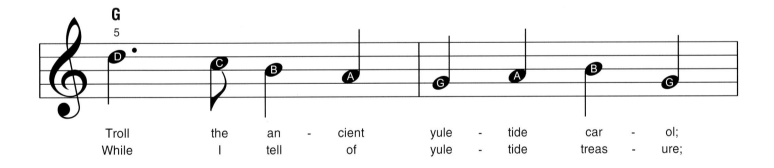

Troll the an - cient yule - tide car - ol;
While I tell of yule - tide treas - ure;

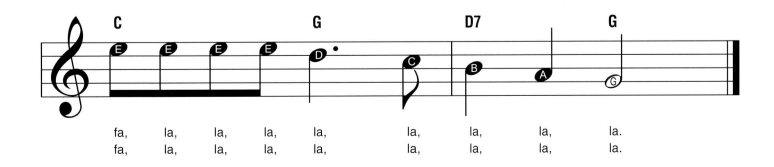

fa, la, la, la, la, la, la, la, la.
fa, la, la, la, la, la, la, la, la.

Angels We Have Heard on High

This traditional carol is known by the long "Gloria" in the chorus. It's 18 notes long!
Hold the half note for a full two beats before the eighth notes lead into the next measure.
There is lots of repetition in this carol, so study the phrases carefully before playing.

Joyfully

Traditional French Carol

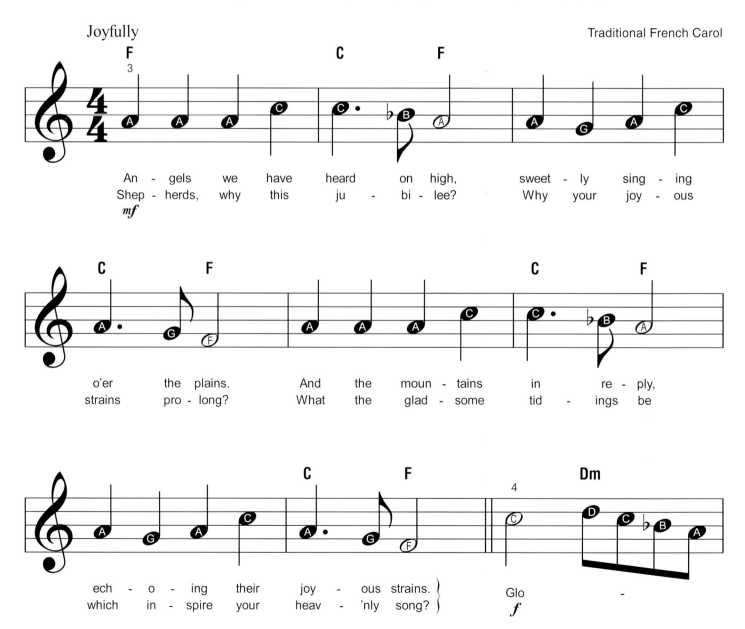

An - gels we have heard on high, sweet - ly sing - ing
Shep - herds, why this ju - bi - lee? Why your joy - ous

o'er the plains. And the moun - tains in re - ply,
strains pro - long? What the glad - some tid - ings be

ech - o - ing their joy - ous strains. Glo -
which in - spire your heav - 'nly song?

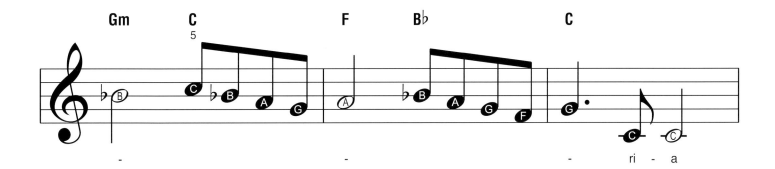

\- \- \- ri - a

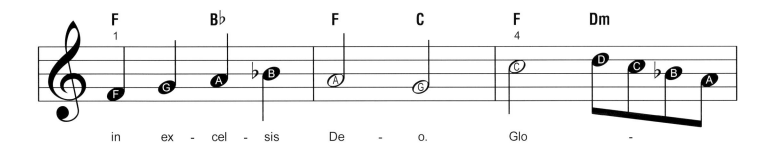

in ex - cel - sis De - o. Glo -

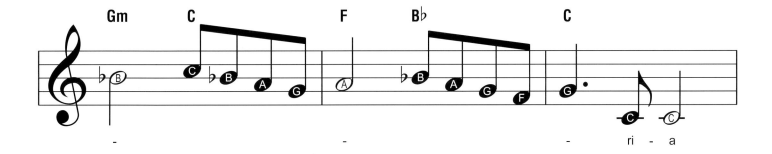

\- \- \- ri - a

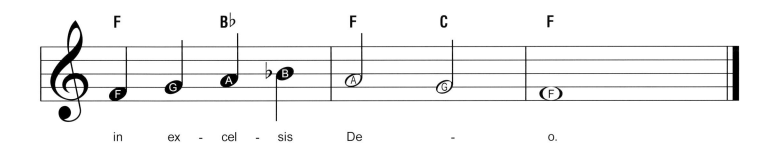

in ex - cel - sis De - o.

Time Signature

A time signature provides two important pieces of information. The top number indicates how many beats are in each measure. The bottom number indicates the type of note that gets one beat. Up to this point, the songs in this book have had the number 4 on the bottom.

The following rhythm example has $\frac{6}{8}$ as the time signature. Here there are six beats in a measure. The eighth note gets one beat.

The answer to Rudolph's question is "both." An eighth note can be half a beat long whenever the bottom number in the time signature is 4. But in $\frac{6}{8}$ time, the eighth note gets one beat. Not only that, but in $\frac{6}{8}$ time a quarter note gets two beats. One thing never changes – two eighth notes always equal one quarter note.

Here are some rhythms to clap and count in $\frac{6}{8}$.

I thought an eighth note is half a beat long. Now you say an eighth note gets one beat. I'm confused! Which is it?

I Saw Three Ships

Clap and count the rhythm before playing this carol. You might want to write in the rhythm below the notes.

Traditional English Carol

Maze

Help Santa put his gift under the tree.

Changing Meter

Sometimes a time signature can change within a song. This can seem tricky, but you will find this clearly marked. Remember which note gets the beat and notice how many beats per measure.

Practice the excerpt below from "Here We Come A-Wassailling." In this example, you are moving from **6/8** to **4/4**. Clap and count as well as sing the melody as you master this.

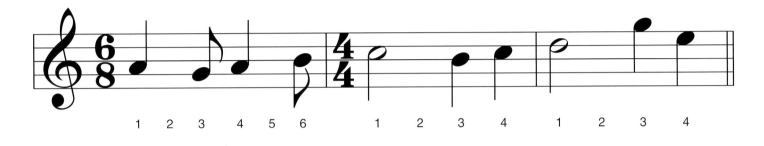

The carol moves back to **6/8** in the measure under the 1st ending bracket. Change from counting "1-2-3-4" back to "1-2-3-4-5-6." Take the repeat sign to play the second verse.

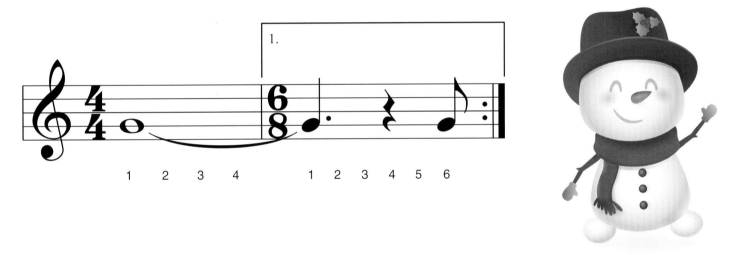

After the second verse you do not change to **6/8** meter; but continue counting four beats to the end.

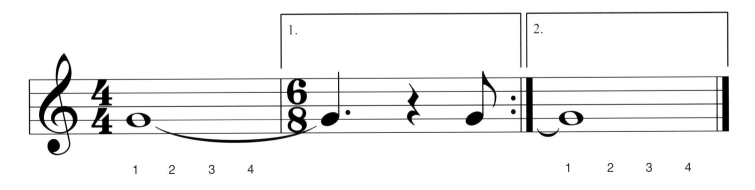

Here We Come A-Wassailing

Traditional

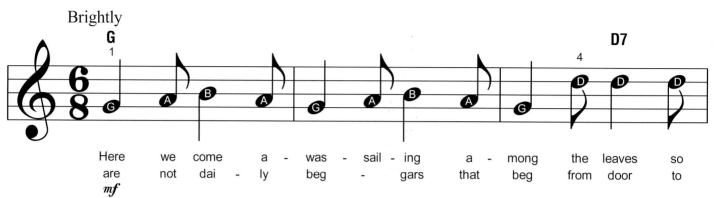

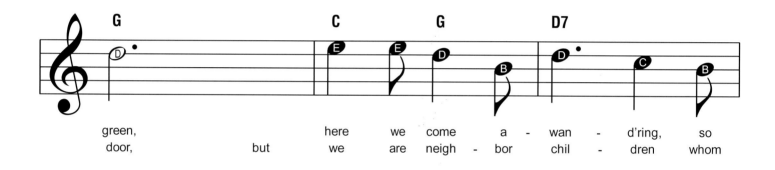

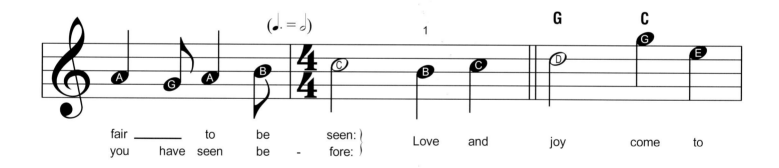

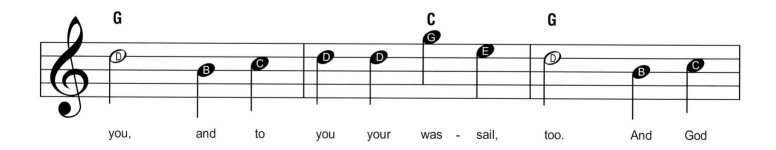

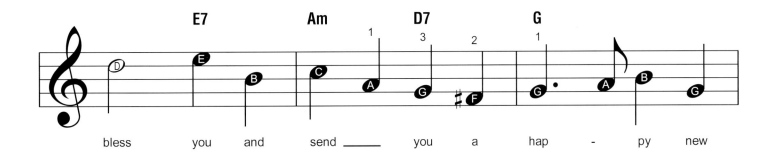

bless you and send ____ you a hap - py new

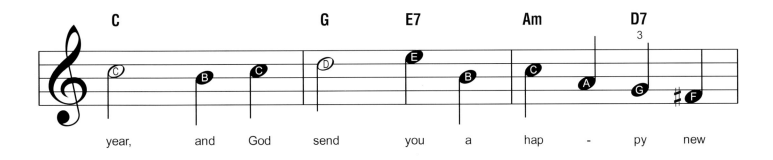

year, and God send you a hap - py new

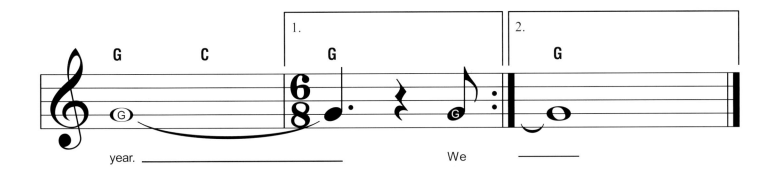

year. _____ We ____

Playing and singing carols together is a long-time holiday tradition. Maybe you've already played some of the carols in this book with friends and family. Playing **duets** (two people playing together) at the keyboard is a challenge and great fun.

Our last carol, "We Wish You a Merry Christmas" is a duet. Play the primo (first) part and ask a partner to join you playing the secondo (second) part. Be sure to set a steady tempo before you begin. For even more fun, switch parts with your partner!

We Wish You a Merry Christmas
(Duet)

Traditional English Folksong

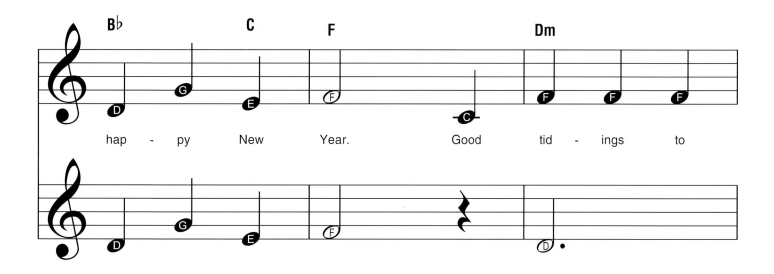

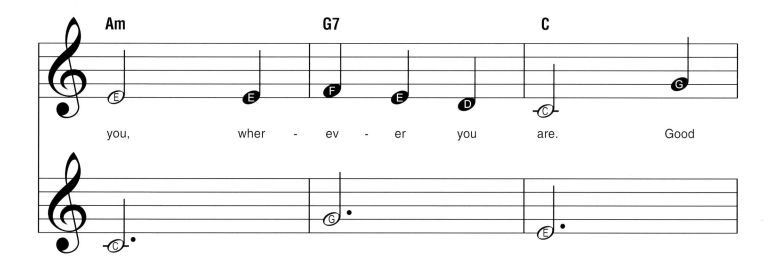

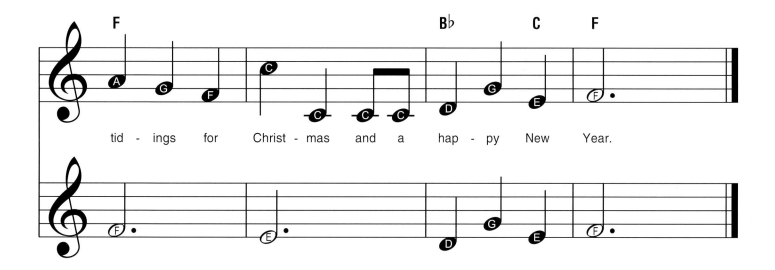

Answer Key

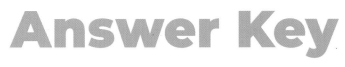

p. 5 - Notes on the Staff

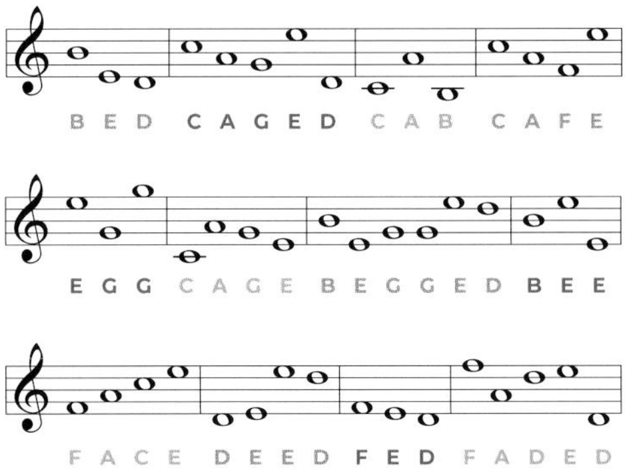

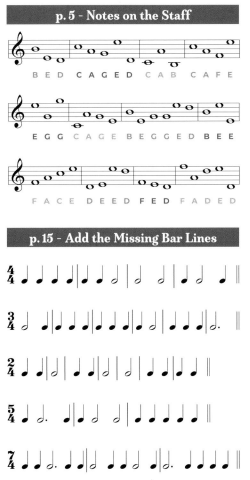

B E D C A G E D C A B C A F E
E G G C A G E B E G G E D B E E
F A C E D E E D F E D F A D E D

p. 15 - Add the Missing Bar Lines

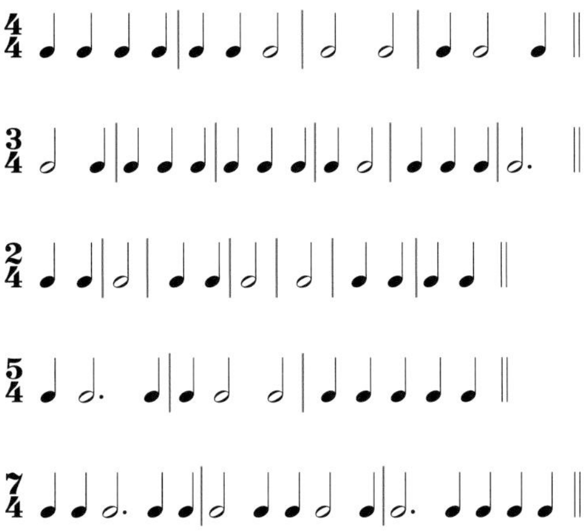

4/4
3/4
2/4
5/4
7/4

p. 28 - Sharp or Flat?

1.) F♯
2.) D♭
3.) A♭
4.) C♯
5.) E♭
6.) D♯
7.) E♭
8.) B♭
9.) F♯
10.) G♯

p. 40 - Crossword Fun

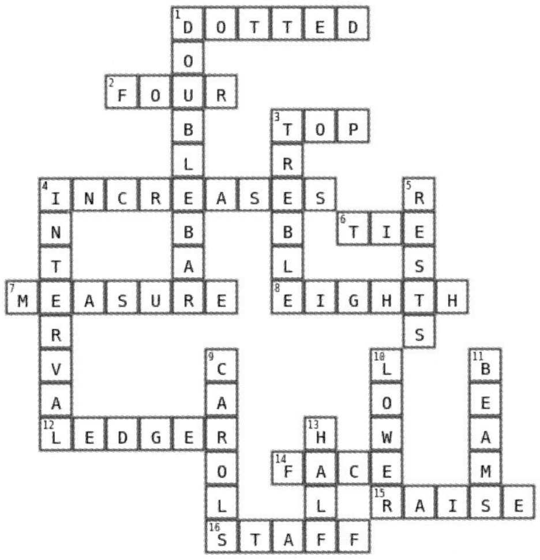

1 DOTTED
1 DOUBLE BAR LINES
2 FOUR
3 TOP
3 TREBLE
4 INCREASES
4 INTERVAL
5 RESTS
6 TIE
7 MEASURE
8 EIGHTH
9 CAROL
10 LOW
11 BEAM
12 LEDGER
13 HALF
14 FACE
15 RAISE
16 STAFF

p. 42 - Music Math

2.) 4 + 4 = 8
3.) 1 + 1 + 1 = 3
4.) 2 + 2 + 1 = 5
5.) 4 + 1 + 2= 7
6.) T
7.) T
8.) T
9.) T
10.) F

p. 49 - Rhythm Match

2.) Silent Night
3.) O Come, All Ye Faithful
4.) What Child Is This?
5.) Jolly Old St. Nicholas
6.) Up on the Housetop
7.) The Holly and the Ivy
8.) Away in a Manger

p. 52 - Playing by Ear

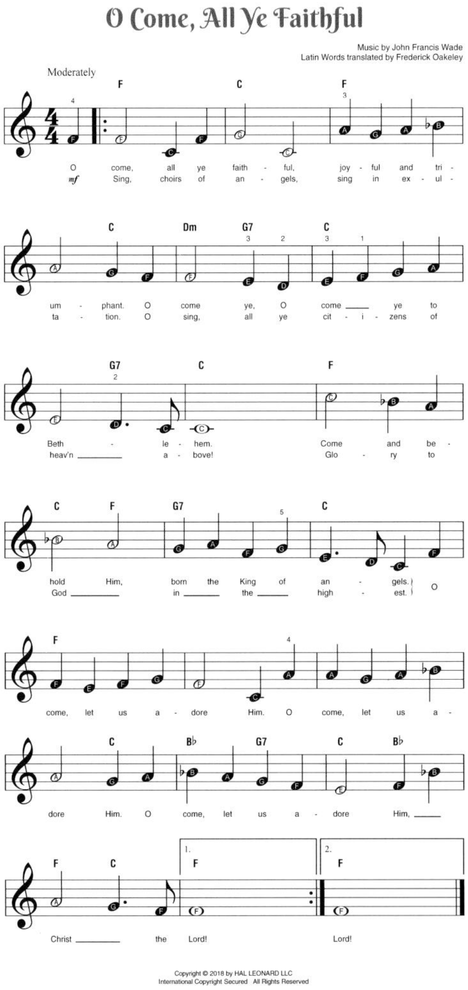

O Come, All Ye Faithful
Music by John Francis Wade
Latin Words translated by Frederick Oakeley
Moderately
F C F C Dm G7 C G7 C F C F G7 C F C B♭ G7 C B♭ F C F F
O come, all ye faith - ful, joy - ful and tri - um - phant. O come ye, O come ye to Beth - le - hem. Come and be - hold Him, born the King of an - gels.
Sing, choirs of an - gels, sing in ex - ul - ta - tion. O sing, all ye cit - i - zens of heav'n a - bove! Glo - ry to God in the high - est.
O come, let us a - dore Him. O come, let us a - dore Him. O come, let us a - dore Him, Christ the Lord! Lord!
Copyright © 2018 by HAL LEONARD LLC
International Copyright Secured All Rights Reserved

p. 56 - Word Search

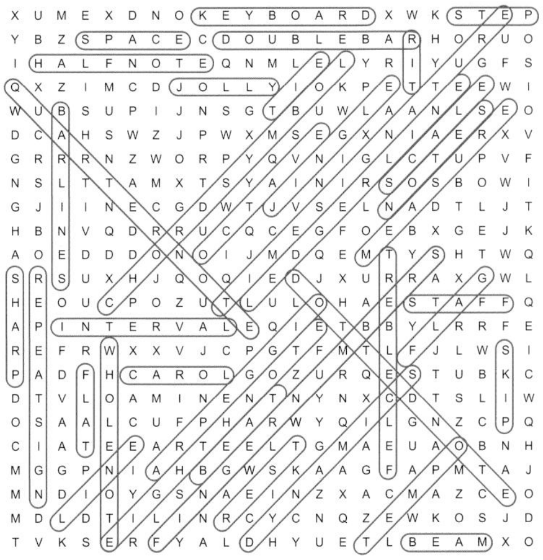

X U M E X D N O K E Y B O A R D X W K S T E P
Y B Z S P A C E C D O U B L E B A R H O R U O
I H A L F N O T E Q N M L E L Y R I Y U G F S
Q X Z I M C D J O L L Y I O K P E T T E E W I
W U B S U P I J N S G T B U W L A A N L S E O
D C A H S W Z J P W X M S E G X N I A E R X V
G R R R N Z W O R P Y Q V N I G L C T U P V F
N S L T T A M X T S Y A I N I R S O S B O W I
G J I I N E C G D W T J V S E L N A D T L J T
H B N V Q D R R U C Q C E G F O E B X G E J K
A O E D D D O N O I J M D Q E M T Y S H T W Q
S R S U X H J Q O Q I E D J X U R R A X G W L
H E O U C P O Z U T L U L O H A E S T A F F Q
A P I N T E R V A L E Q I E T B B Y L R R F E
R E F R W X X V J C P G T F M T L F J L W S I
P A D F H C A R O L G O Z U R Q E S T U B K C
D T V L O A M I N E N T N Y N X C D T S L I W
O S A A L C U F P H A R W Y Q I L G N Z C P Q
C I A T E E A R T E E L T G M A E U A O B N H
M G G P N I A H B G W S K A A G F A P M T A J
M N D I O Y G S N A E I N Z X A C M A Z C E O
M D L D T I L I N R C Y C N Q Z E W K O S J D
T V K S E R F Y A L D H Y U E T L B E A M X O

p. 59 - Note Reading Challenge

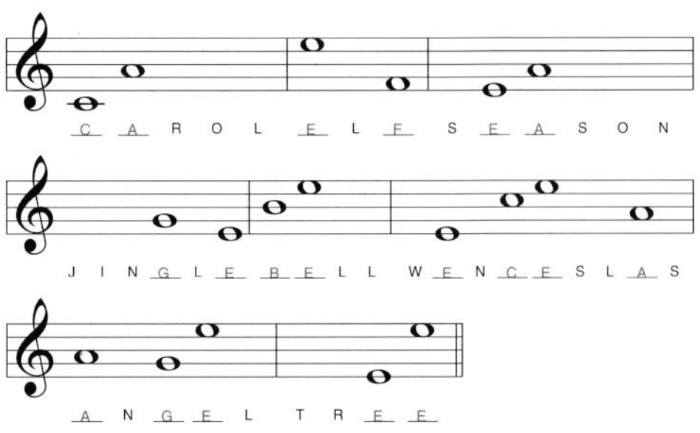

C A R O L E L F S E A S O N
J I N G L E B E L L W E N C E S L A S
A N G E L T R E E

p. 66 - Maze

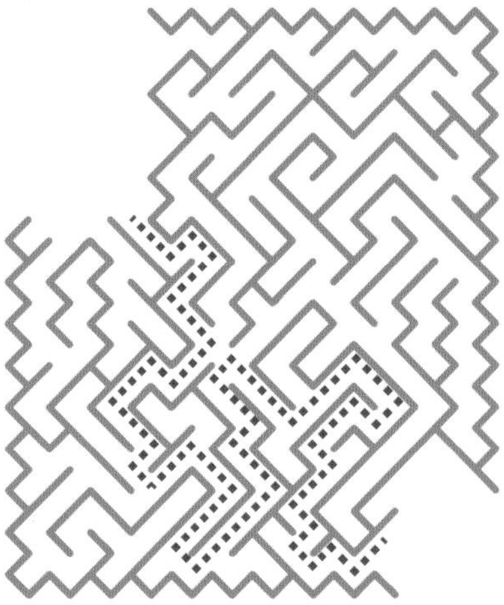

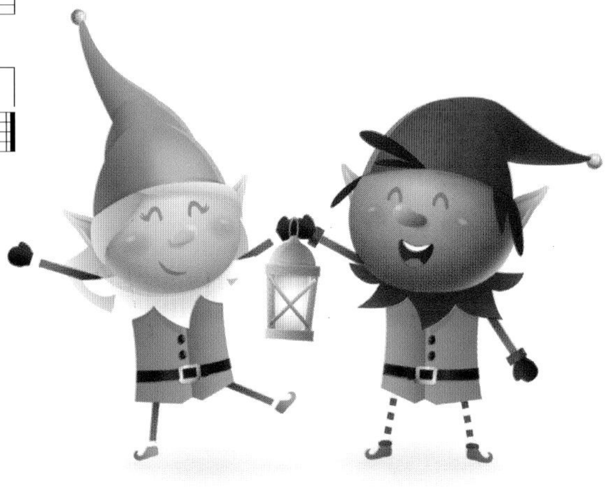